Serious FUN!

Work & Play with Charles & Ray
EAMES

Christy Hale

A NEAL PORTER BOOK HOLIDAY HOUSE

For Neal

Neal Porter Books
An imprint of Holiday House Publishing, Inc.

Text and illustrations copyright © 2026 by Christy Hale
All rights reserved. No part of this book may be reproduced, transmitted, or stored in an information retrieval system in any form or by any means, graphic, electronic, or mechanical, including photocopying, taping, and recording, without prior written permission from the publisher. Additionally, no part of this book may be used or reproduced in any manner for the purpose of training artificial intelligence technologies or systems, nor for text and data mining.
HOLIDAY HOUSE is registered in the U.S. Patent and Trademark Office.
Printed and bound in November 2025 at C&C Offset, Shenzhen, China.
The artwork for this book was made using collage, print, and line.
Book design by Christy Hale
www.holidayhouse.com
First Edition
1 3 5 7 9 10 8 6 4 2

Library of Congress Cataloging-in-Publication Data is available.

ISBN: 978-0-8234-5660-4 (hardcover)
EU Authorized Representative: HackettFlynn Ltd, 36 Cloch Choirneal,
Balrothery, Co. Dublin, K32 C942, Ireland. EU@walkerpublishinggroup.com

"Take your pleasure seriously."

The twentieth-century design duo Charles and Ray Eames had serious fun experimenting and solving problems. They followed their interests wherever they led, not limiting themselves to any one design category. Work and play merged in their collaborations on furniture design, architecture, textile design, graphic design, photography, film, multiscreen media, exhibition design, and even toy design. In every process Charles and Ray were eager learners.

When Charles was three, Halley's Comet blazed across the sky and lit him with wonder. Charles was curious about everything. He observed and he sketched.

At three, Ray was already a fashion designer. Ray cut out colored shapes and drew tiny details.

Charles was eight when his father, a railway security officer, was shot by a train robber and had to retire. At ten, Charles began his first job at a print shop. After his father's death five years later, the family relied on Charles. He worked as a steel laborer, full time in the summer and on weekends during the school year. Still, Charles was the top student and the president of his class.

Ray's father, a manager for a vaudeville theater, introduced her to performers, including a Russian ballerina who taught dance. Ray practiced and practiced, learning the discipline needed to accomplish anything great.

Ray also filled notebooks with her drawings and joined the school art club.

Charles found his father's photography equipment. He experimented, played, and made discoveries. Looking through the lens of a camera, Charles saw the world in new ways.

Ray's father loved toys, games, and being in nature. He died unexpectedly when Ray was a teenager, but his sense of fun stayed with her. Ray greeted life with zest.

Drawing led Charles to architecture. In his job at the steel mill, Charles used drawings to show engineering solutions and create patterns. This earned him an architectural scholarship at Washington University in St. Louis, but he was asked to leave the program after two years. His opinions about architecture were too new, too *modern* to be accepted by his professors.

Drawing led Ray to painting. Though she graduated from the Bennett School for Girls in fashion design she soon moved to New York City to study art. Ray was a founder of the American Abstract Artists and exhibited in the first group show. Unlike traditional painters, she used lines, shapes, and colors to express emotion. Like Charles, Ray's ideas were *modern*.

"Eventually everything connects—people, ideas, objects."

Modern ideas led each to Cranbrook Academy of Art in Michigan, a laboratory of experimentation. Students moved between studying architecture, furniture design, metalworking, weaving, and ceramics. Charles was the head of the Industrial Design department.

Though Ray signed up for weaving classes, she spent most of her time in the design studio. There Ray met Charles.

The Organic Chair was created at Cranbrook. There, Charles met architect Eero Saarinen and they teamed up to enter the Museum of Modern Art Organic Design for Home Furnishings competition. They wanted to design chairs for mass production, chairs that everyone could afford, chairs that didn't need padding for comfort. They planned something new, molding plywood into curves that fit the human body.
Ray worked on the drawings.

The chair won first place and—*kazam!*—Charles and Ray fell in love.

Though the chair succeeded in the competition, it failed its goal. The plywood splintered from the stress of bending. The chair could not be manufactured. Charles and Ray determined to learn from mistakes. They wanted to make **the best** designs **for the most** people **for the least** cost. They married and became partners in love and work. They moved to Los Angeles and started experimenting.

In their apartment, they rigged up a contraption to bend plywood. Using electrical coils, a bicycle pump, and an inflatable bag, they forced layer upon layer of thin glue-coated plywood into plaster molds. The glue dried, the pressure released, and like magic, their Kazam! machine made a new form.

They worked and played—

bending, **twisting,** **cutting holes,**

exploring possibilities.

Ray Eames, 1943 Plywood Sculpture

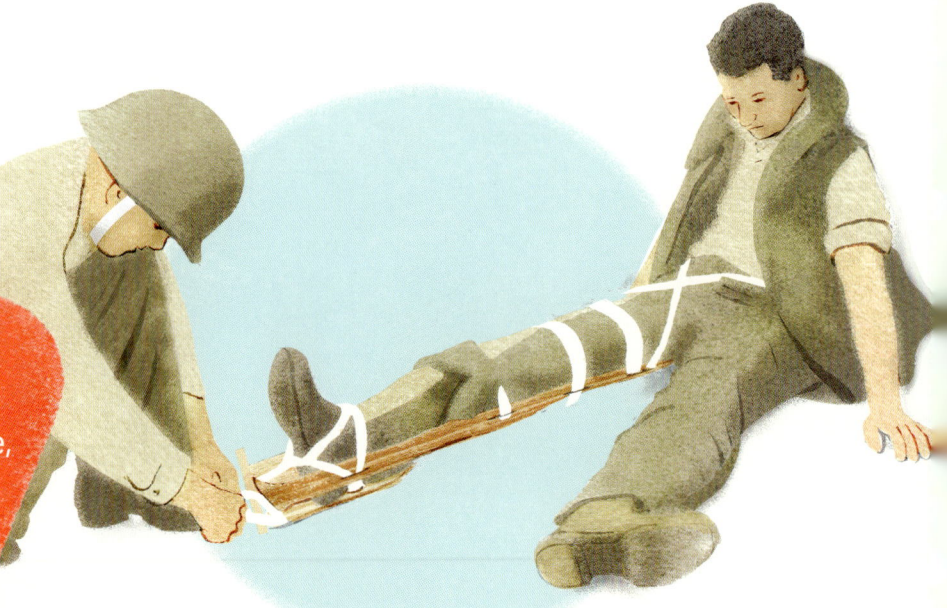

During World War II, the metal splints used on the wounded were making injuries worse. Charles and Ray's experiments with the Kazam! machine taught them how wood and glue respond to heat and pressure. They designed an inexpensive, lightweight plywood splint molded to the human leg that offered better support. They cut holes where medics could wrap bandages and discovered that those holes relieved the stress in the bent plywood.

Charles and Ray learned by doing.

"Never delegate understanding."

Using the Eameses' prototypes, the U.S. Navy produced 150,000 leg splints; also arm splints, body litters, pilot seats, and other aircraft parts. Their contract with the Navy gave them access to more materials, better technology, and manufacturing facilities. Charles and Ray continued their experiments with furniture and after much hard work produced the Lounge Chair Wood (LCW), honored by *Time* magazine as the Best Design of the 20th Century.

Charles and Ray did not work alone to produce the splints and furniture. They teamed up with others in a big old repair garage that became the Eames Office.

They designed for different needs, making chairs with arms, chairs that rocked, chairs that stacked, office chairs, rolling chairs, lounge chairs, and more. Experimentation never stopped.

Ray combined the lines, shapes, and colors of abstract art with her love of fashion to design fabrics.

Ray entered "Cross Patch" in the MoMA textile design competition.

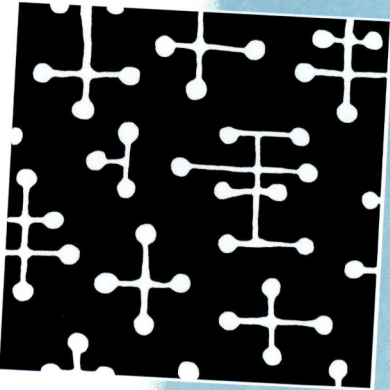

The "Dot" pattern remains Ray's most well-known textile design.

Ray designed abstract covers for twenty-six issues of *Arts & Architecture*, a magazine focused on innovative art, architecture, music, and film. Both Charles and Ray worked closely on the magazine with publisher and editor, John Entenza.

Charles was one of eight architects John Entenza chose for the Case Study House Program, sponsored by *Arts & Architecture* to help with the postwar housing shortage. Sample homes for average families were designed and built using inexpensive materials, modern technology, and a rapid schedule.

Charles and Ray designed a home and studio overlooking their favorite picnic spot, which you can still visit.

Young designers could construct anything they imagined with "The Toy," a kit of colorful geometric panels.

Playing with the possibilities of molded plywood led to children's furniture and a group of animals. The two-part elephant had complicated curves!

Charles and Ray created toys that encouraged imaginative open-ended play, freethinking, and problem-solving.

Building with the "House of Cards" developed an understanding of structure. The deck of slotted cards featured varied textures, colors, and patterns.

"Toys are not really as innocent as they look. Toys and games are the preludes to serious ideas."

Charles and Ray's "Solar Do-Nothing Machine" designed for Alcoa, the Aluminum Company of America, in 1957, was one of the first uses of solar power to produce electricity. Sunlight reflected onto cells became a battery, activating the pulleys and turning the wheels of this colorful toy.

When a friend loaned Charles and Ray a movie projector, they rented a movie camera, then after work, made films for fun. Altogether, they created more than 125 films. Their early films focused on toys. Charles and Ray had a large collection of kites, masks, dolls, trains, tops, and more.

Tops (1969) shows over 100 spinning tops from around the world, celebrating one of the most ancient toys.

Toccata for Toy Trains (1957) features antique trains, horse-drawn carriages, automobiles, dolls, and windup figures moving to music by Elmer Bernstein.

Charles and Ray's films took complicated ideas and broke down the information into simple forms. Cartoon animation made computers understandable to the average person.

The Information Machine (1958) was the Eameses' first commissioned film, made for the IBM Pavilion at the Brussels World's Fair. The Eameses showed how people have created tools and systems for collecting information and problem-solving since ancient times, leading up to the development of the computer.

Powers of Ten (1958) opens showing two people enjoying a picnic. The overhead camera moves farther and farther away. Up and up, it continues to the edge of the universe! Then the direction changes. The camera comes closer and closer, magnifying each view into the molecules of a hand! The film shows the importance of scale.

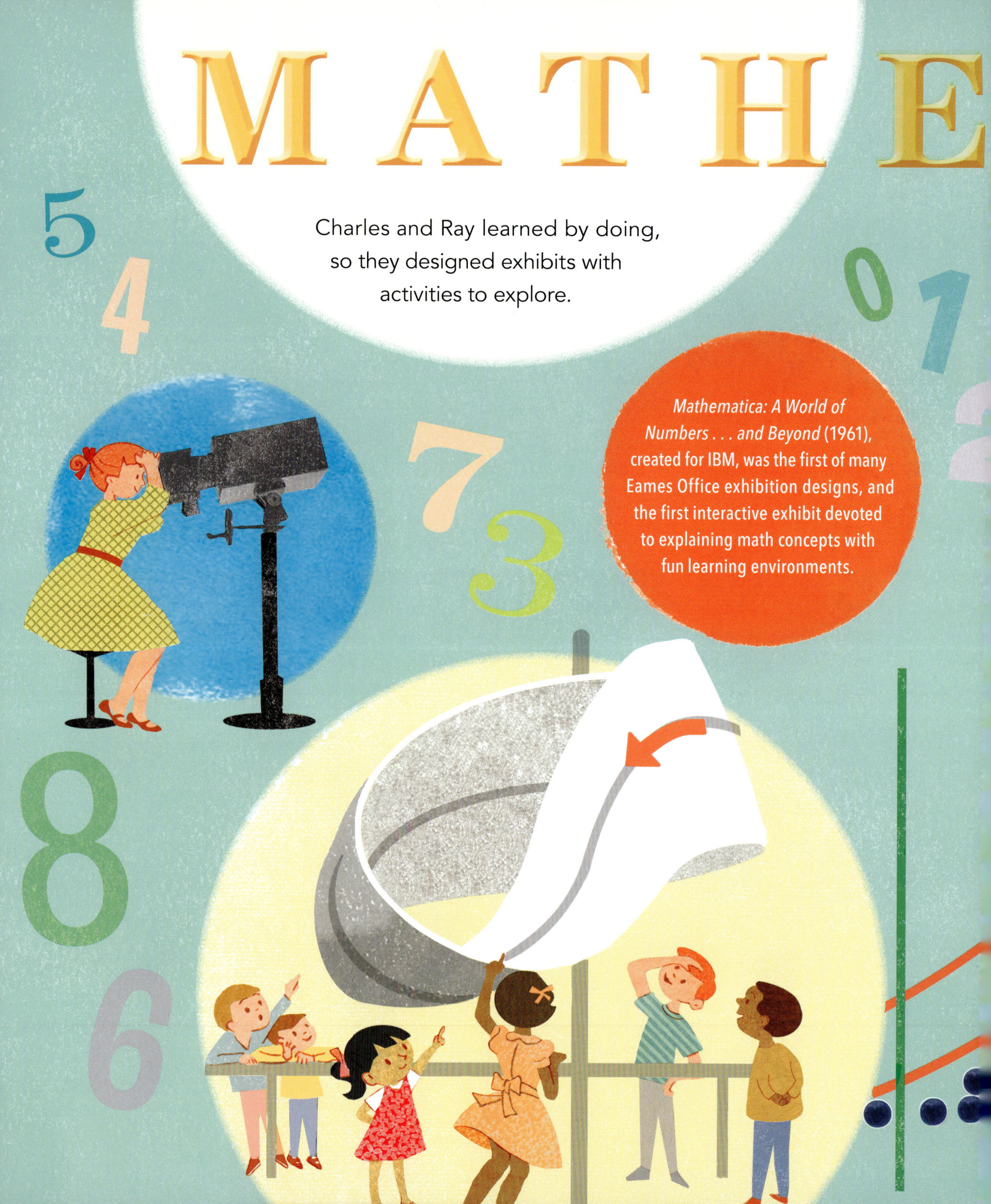

MATHE

Charles and Ray learned by doing, so they designed exhibits with activities to explore.

Mathematica: A World of Numbers . . . and Beyond (1961), created for IBM, was the first of many Eames Office exhibition designs, and the first interactive exhibit devoted to explaining math concepts with fun learning environments.

"When a man assumes a public trust, he should consider him[self]

"Freedom of speech is ever the symptom, as well as the effect of a good government."

"Where the press is free and every man able to read, all is safe."

"Early to bed and early to rise, makes a man healthy, wealthy, and wise."

"A little rebellion now and then is a good thing, and as necessary in the political world as storms in the physical."

"There has never been nor ever will be any such thing as a good war or a bad peace."

"... nothing is ours which another may deprive us of. Hence the inestimable value of intellectual pleasures."

"They who can give up essential liberty to obtain a little temporary safety deserve neither liberty nor safety."

"Reason and free inquiry are the only effectual agents against error."

"as public property."

"Beyond the age of information is the age of choices."

The traveling exhibit *The World of Franklin and Jefferson* (1975–1977) was Charles and Ray's largest project and their final exhibition design. Images, objects, and words filled seven thousand feet of museum space, celebrating the American Bicentennial and examining the connections between Founding Fathers Benjamin Franklin and Thomas Jefferson and their contributions to independence.

architecture

Charles trained as an architect and designed houses and churches before teaming up with Ray. Case Study House No. 8, the Eames House, is their most notable completed work together. Charles saw structure in all their projects. He said, "If you start out in architecture, then go on to furniture and then to toys and films, essentially it's the same problem."

painting

Ray trained as an abstract painter and showed her work in New York City before meeting Charles. In all their collaborations—furniture, toys, films, and more—Ray contributed her sense of form and color, affecting the look of every Eames Office creation. She said, "I never gave up painting, I just changed my palette."

drawing

From their earliest years, both drew and drew, laying the foundation for their future work. In their teens, Charles drafted engineering patterns and drew cartoons; Ray designed fashions and posters.

> "The most important thing is that you love what you are doing, and the second, that you are not afraid of where your next idea will lead."

> "Everything hangs on something else."

photography

The Eameses took hundreds of thousands of photographs. They documented their own designs and studied natural forms and everyday objects. Their photographs reveal the "uncommon beauty of common things."

Hang-It-All (1953) for hanging things, constructed of wood and rubber-coated steel wire.

furniture

Charles and Ray met through their efforts in furniture design. The two continued designing furniture for forty years, exploring materials, creating affordable, mass-produced, formfitting chairs for the home, schools, stadiums, and airports, as well as storage units, cabinets, tables, lounges, benches, stools, room dividers, and more.

toys

The Eameses found inspiration in their international collection of toys, masks, tops, and trains. They began producing toys for the children in their lives—colorful shapes to assemble, slotted pattern cards to interlock—encouraging creativity and many hours of open-ended building play.

graphics

The Eames Office designed graphics for magazine covers, advertising, posters, invitations, timelines, business cards, game boards, sales displays, exhibitions, and films.

models

Charles and Ray created countless models of designs to test their ideas and explore improvements. "What works good is better than what looks good because what works good lasts."

masks

They made masks—large bird, fish, and animal costumes for both children and adults.

textiles

Ray submitted four textile patterns to MoMA's 1947 competition for fabric design and received an honorable mention. Two of the designs were produced during Ray's lifetime and additional designs were later made available, and those fabrics are still in production today.

fashion

Ray's interest in fashion began with the creation of her first paper dolls at age three. She studied fashion design until the 1930s. When Ray planned her own wardrobe, she kept function in mind, adding lots of pockets for handy access to useful tools and other odds and ends, the small wonders that caught her eye—stones, fossils, shells, little scraps of paper, and fabric became her inspiration. Ray designed clothing for Charles, church choir robes, and uniforms for IBM staff at the 1964 New York World's Fair.

films

For Charles and Ray, film was a way to experiment and educate by making complicated ideas accessible. They made 125 short films, exploring their interests while also combining their love of photography and theater.

multiscreen

Multiscreen shows compressed information, allowing viewers to make their own connections. In *Glimpses of the U.S.A.* (1959), two thousand images flashed on seven thirty-foot screens showing the diversity and complexity of American life.

exhibitions

World's Fair and museum exhibition designs provided the Eameses an arena for educating the public on a variety of subjects.

Charles & Ray

Charles Ormond Eames Jr. (1907–1978) was three when Halley's Comet streaked across the sky, searing his first memory.

The family lived in St. Louis, Missouri. After his father's retirement and subsequent death, Charles helped support his mother and older sister with a variety of jobs. Working for manufacturers and engineers fed his curiosity about mechanics and also sparked his interest in architecture.

His father also had been an amateur photographer. Charles explored the old camera equipment and chemicals and began a lifelong love of photography.

In 1925, he enrolled in the Washington University in St. Louis architecture classes and was soon the best at design problem-solving. Still, Charles was asked to leave the program because his ideas were considered too modern.

In 1929, Charles married Catherine Woermann. Lucia Eames was born in 1930. The marriage ended in divorce in 1941.

In 1930, Charles began an architectural practice in St. Louis. One of his buildings was noticed by architect Eliel Saarinen, the president of Cranbrook Academy of Art. He invited Charles to come to the school for further architecture study.

Bernice Alexandra Kaiser Eames (1912–1988) was nicknamed "Ray-Ray" by her brother. The name stuck, and later she officially changed her name.

The family lived in Sacramento, California. Her father, a traveling "mesmerist" in his youth, became a vaudeville theater manager. Both parents loved entertainment, from classical to popular, including film. Ray's early years were filled with art, dance, nature outings, and picnics. The family enjoyed life!

Her father died suddenly in 1929. In 1931, Ray graduated from high school, studied briefly at Sacramento Junior College, then with her mother, moved to New York to be closer to her brother studying at West Point. Ray attended the nearby Bennett School for Girls, graduating in 1933 with a degree in fashion design.

Ray moved to Manhattan and began six years of study with the abstract expressionist Hans Hofmann, learning about structure and color in painting.

In late 1939, Ray moved to Florida to nurse her dying mother, who passed in the spring of 1940. Ray was at another point of change. At a friend's suggestion, she went to Cranbrook Academy of Art.

Charles and Ray first met through their team efforts on the organic chair design. Collaboration defined their partnership, and later, expanded to include the work of the Eames Office. Problems were best solved with the contributions of different skill sets.

They studied the needs of those they designed for—the shape of a leg for splints, sitting posture for formfitting chairs. "The role of the designer is that of a very good, thoughtful host, anticipating the needs of his guests."

They accepted constraints "of price, of size, of strength, of balance, of surface, of time, and so forth. Each problem has its own peculiar list."

Both were curious and followed their interests, trying things in multiple ways, playing—making connections, believing that "real learning comes from primary experiences." Only then could their designs flow from that learning.

Charles and Ray made multiple models and life-sized mock-ups to try out their ideas and make adjustments. They were constantly redesigning and rethinking projects to improve them.

Splints, furniture, textiles, graphics, architecture, toys, films, and exhibition spaces—Charles and Ray believed in the power of design to improve the quality of life. Through mass production and media, they made their innovations and ideas accessible and many of their designs endure to this day.

> "We worked very hard at that—enjoying ourselves. We didn't let anything interfere with what we were doing—our hard work. That in itself was a great pleasure."

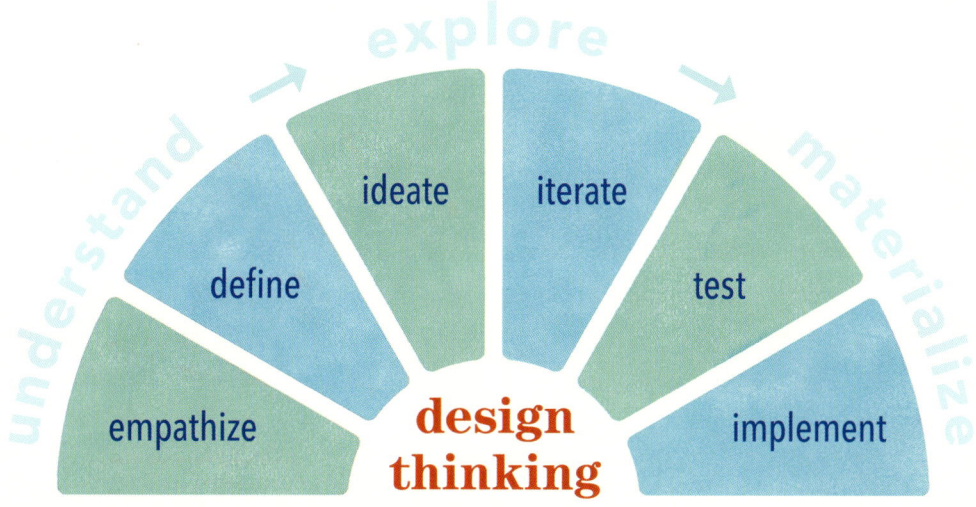

In the 1990s, Charles and Ray's philosophy of "learning by doing" was reframed by David Kelley and Tim Brown (of IDEO) as "design thinking."

LEARN MORE

Books

Demetrios, Eames. *Eames: Beautiful Details*. Los Angeles: AMMO Books, 2012.

Demetrios, Eames. *An Eames Primer*. New York: Rizzoli, 2013.

Neuhart, John, Marilyn Neuhart, and Ray Eames. *Eames Design: The Work of the Office of Charles and Ray Eames*. New York: Abrams, 1989.

Films

Eames: The Architect and the Painter. Directed and produced by Jason Cohn and Bill Jersey. New York: First Run Features, 2011.

The Films of Charles & Ray Eames, vol. 1–6. Los Angeles: Eames Office, 2005.

Websites

Eames Institute
    www.eamesinstitute.org

Eames Office
    www.eamesoffice.com

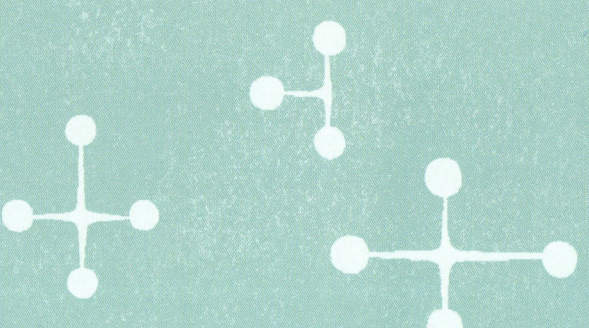

QUOTATION SOURCES

p. 3: "Take your pleasure seriously." Charles Eames in a speech for the American Philosophical Society, Philadelphia, PA, 1974.

p. 10: "Eventually everything . . . ideas, objects." Charles Eames narration from a film on the "ESU" storage system, 1961, quoted from Ralph Caplan, *Connections: The Work of Charles and Ray Eames* (Los Angeles: UCLA Art Council, 1976), p. 15.

p. 12: "the best for the most for the least." Charles Eames. Demetrios, Eames. *Eames: Beautiful Details*. Los Angeles: AMMO Books, 2012, p. 62.

p. 15: "Never delegate understanding." Charles Eames. *Eames: The Architect and the Painter*. Directed and produced by Jason Cohn and Bill Jersey. New York: First Run Features, 2011.

p. 19: "We work . . . the next." Charles Eames. Charles Eliot Norton Lectures in Poetry #5, Harvard University, March 29, 1971.

p. 27: "Toys are not . . . serious ideas." Charles Eames. O'Connell, James B. "A Visit with Charles Eames," *Think 27*, no. 4 (April 1961): pp. 7–9.

p. 33: "Let the fun out of the bag." Charles Eames. *Mathematica: A World of Numbers . . . and Beyond* (1961), Museum of Science and Industry, Chicago, IL. https://www.eamesinstitute.org/collection/artifacts/mathematica.

p. 35: "Beyond the age . . . of choices." Charles Eames. "Making Connections" (unpublished outline and lecture notes, p. 2, International Design Conference in Aspen, CO, June 1978).

p. 36: "If you start . . . same problem." Charles Eames. Shapiro, Harriet. "Eames on Eames," *Intellectual Digest* 3 (August 1973): pp. 34–37.

p. 36: "I never . . . my palette." Ray Eames, 1982. Demetrios, Eames. *Changing Her Palette: Paintings by Ray Eames*. Santa Monica: The Eames Office, 2000.

p. 36: "The most important . . . idea will lead." Charles Eames. Hartman, Carla, and Eames Demetrios, editors. *100 Quotes by Charles Eames*. Santa Monica: The Eames Office, 2007.

p. 36: "Everything hangs on something else." Ray Eames. Interview by Ruth Bowman for the Archives of American Art, Venice, CA, July 28, 1980.

p. 36: "the uncommon beauty of common things." Charles Eames. Demetrios, Eames. *An Eames Primer*. New York: Rizzoli, 2013, p. 145.

p. 37: "What works . . . good lasts." Ray Eames. Neuhart, John, Marilyn Neuhart, and Ray Eames. *Eames Design: The Work of the Office of Charles and Ray Eames*. New York: Abrams, 1989.

p. 39: "The role . . . his guests." Charles Eames. Charles Eliot Norton Lectures in Poetry #1, Harvard University, October 26, 1970.

p. 39: "of price . . . peculiar list." Charles Eames. "Design Q & A (1972)," July 23, 2013. https://www.youtube.com/watch?v=bmgxDCujTUw.

p. 39: "real learning . . . primary experiences." Charles Eames. Charles Eliot Norton Lectures in Poetry #1, Harvard University, October 26, 1970.

p. 39: "We worked . . . great pleasure." Ray Eames. Demetrios, Eames, and Carla Hartman, editors. *Essential Eames: Words & Pictures*. Weil am Rein, Germany: Vitra Design Museum, 2017, p. 128.